If the
Earth....
were a few feet
in diameter

BY JOE MILLER
ARTWORK BY WILSON MCLEAN

If the Earth...
were a few feet
in diameter

THE GREENWICH WORKSHOP PRESS

If the Earth were a
few feet in diameter,
floating a few feet above
a field somewhere,

people would come from
everywhere to marvel at it.

People would walk around it marvelling at its big pools of water, its little pools and the water flowing between.

If the Earth were a few feet in diameter, all of the 332 million cubic miles of water in its oceans, lakes and rivers would amount to a little more than half a gallon.

• • •

The Earth's 5,600 trillion tons of atmosphere would weigh just over an ounce and, breathing normally, you could inhale and exhale it all in three minutes.

• • •

Instead of surrounding the Earth in a blanket 20 miles deep, the atmosphere would be reduced to a band a little more than a tenth of an inch thick.

• • •

All of the world's land could be arranged on a bedspread. The United States would fit on your pillowcase.

• • •

A stack of pennies that would reach to the Earth's center would be worth only $5. A stack worth more than $40 million would be needed to reach to the center of the Earth at its actual size.

• • •

It would take you just a few hours to walk to the Sun, which would be 11 miles away and more than 500 feet in diameter. But you could walk to the Moon in under a minute, as it would be only about 150 feet away, and 16 inches in diameter.

People would marvel at the
bumps on it and the holes in it.
They would marvel at the very
thin layer of gas surrounding
it and the water
suspended in
the gas.

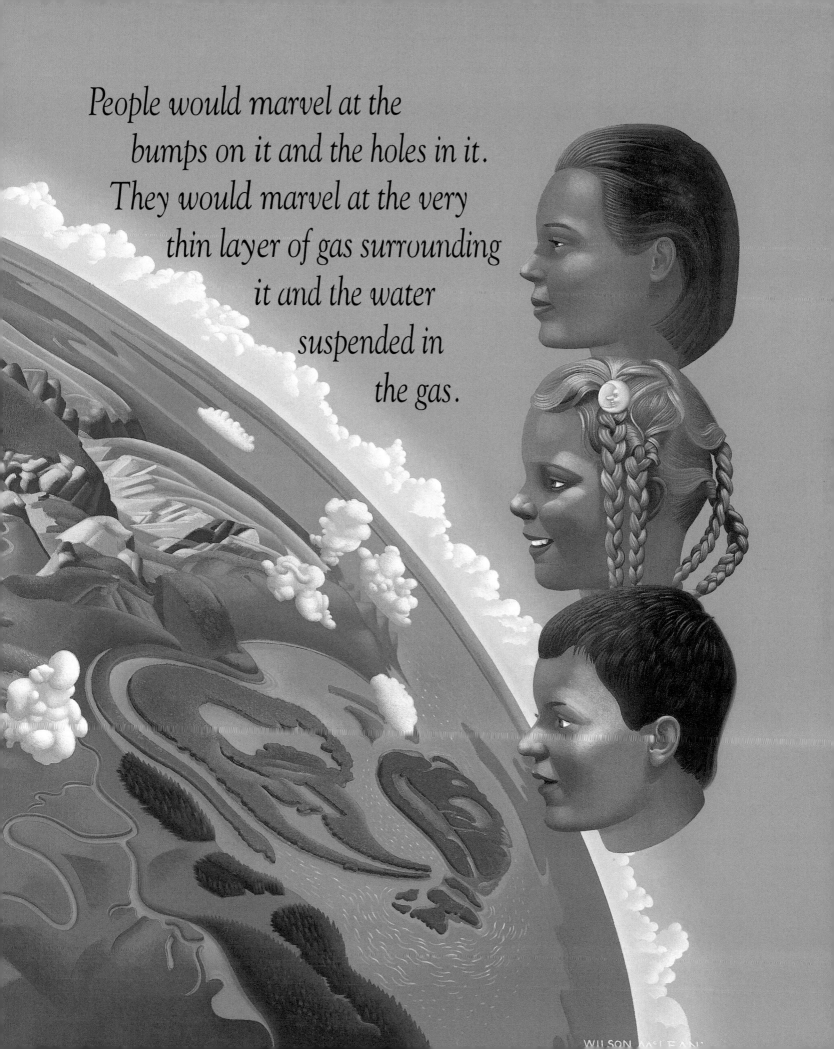

The people would marvel at all the creatures walking around the surface of the ball

Nearly a million and a half different types of plants and animals inhabit the Earth, and those are just the ones we've seen. It is thought that there may be as many as 40 million different species of plants and animals.

• • •

A tablespoon of marshy water may hold millions of the simplest creatures. In a mere tenth of an ounce of soil, there may be three million organisms.

• • •

The tallest plant, the redwood tree, can grow to be over 300 feet tall. That's 300 million times bigger than the smallest plant. Some sub-microscopic algae are no more than a ten-thousandth of an inch long.

• • •

The water that reaches from the oceans' surface to 300 feet deep contains the source of all food for the life that dwells in it. Sixteen percent of the world's animals live in the sea.

• • •

The largest animal in the world is the blue whale, whose weight of 200 tons is 24,560 billion times heavier than the smallest insect—a parisitic wasp that weighs 0.0000002 ounces.

• • •

While some roots may reach lower and some animals may dwell higher, most life on land begins a few feet below the soil's surface and ends at the highest treetops.

and at the creatures in the water.

The people would declare
it as sacred because it was
the only one, and they
would protect it so that it
would not be hurt.

Of all the tales told among the many religions of the world, the most solemn are the creation tales. These sacred stories cast Earth itself as a religious form—the source of all other life forms and powers. In many cultures, "Mother Earth" is one of the oldest and most widespread of religious symbols. Like a woman giving birth to children, so the Earth brings forth life.

• • •

One Japanese creation myth begins with an egg that is half gold, half silver. The gold yolk becomes the bright heavens; the silver white becomes the mountains, clouds and sea.

• • •

In a myth from China, the great man P'an Ku dies and his flesh forms the soil, his bones become the rocks, from his blood run the rivers and seas and from his hair comes all vegetation. His breath becomes the wind, his voice the thunder and his sweat the rain. In a Hindu version of this creation myth, the Earth and sky are formed from the giant Purusha.

• • •

The Indian Minyong myth tells of the original union of the Earth (Sedi) and the sky (Melo). Caught between them were the people and animals, who, afraid of being crushed, beat the sky back until he fled into the heavens.

The ball would be
the greatest
wonder known,

and people would come to
pray to it, to be healed,

Some 60 billion people have lived and died on the Earth since mankind's beginnings. And it is all but certain that no two were ever, or will ever be, identical. The odds against that happening are so great that the number could be written out as 1 followed by more than 9,000 zeros.

• • •

The Earth is about 4.5 billion years old. If that were represented by one year, then life would not even begin until March 29. The first fish would not appear until December 7 and the first amphibians, December 14. The dinosaurs would be born and die between December 15 and December 26. Ape-men would appear at 6:17 p.m. on December 31; Jesus Christ would be born 14 seconds before midnight, and the oldest person alive today would have been born within the last second.

• • •

If we could see the Earth from 300,000 miles out in space, its many pieces of land, swirls of clouds and vast reaches of water would appear to be so small as to resemble some of the countless cells that we are all made of.

• • •

According to some of the best estimates, there are more than 400 million planets in our galaxy alone that bear a rich amount of life on land, but ours is currently the only living world we know.

to gain

knowledge,

to know beauty and to wonder how it could be.

People would
love it, and defend
it with their lives because
they would somehow
know that their lives
could be nothing
without it.

If the Earth
were a few feet
in diameter.

If the Earth were a few feet
in diameter, floating a few feet above
a field somewhere, people would come from
everywhere to marvel at it. People would walk
around it marvelling at its big pools of water, its little
pools and the water flowing between. People would marvel
at the bumps on it and the holes in it. They would marvel at
the very thin layer of gas surrounding it and the water suspended
in the gas. The people would marvel at all the creatures walking
around the surface of the ball and at the creatures in the water.
The people would declare it as sacred because it was the only
one, and they would protect it so that it would not be hurt.
The ball would be the greatest wonder known, and people
would come to pray to it, to be healed, to gain knowledge,
to know beauty and to wonder how it could be. People
would love it, and defend it with their lives because
they would somehow know that their lives
could be nothing without it. If the Earth
were a few feet in diameter.

To the undying memory of Alan Gussow.
—JOE MILLER

•

To Rosemary, whose support and patience are immeasurable.
—WILSON MCLEAN

A GREENWICH WORKSHOP PRESS BOOK
Inquiries should be addressed to The Greenwich Workshop, Inc.,
One Greenwich Place, P.O. Box 875, Shelton, Connecticut 06484-0875.

•

Library of Congress Cataloging-in-Publication Data:
Miller, Joe (Joseph), 1939–
If the earth were a few feet in diameter / by Joe Miller ; artwork by Wilson McLean.   p.   cm.
Summary: The wonders of the world are portrayed in paintings, poetic text, and a
presentation of facts about planet Earth.
ISBN 0-86713-054-7 (alk. paper)
1. Earth—Miscellanea—Juvenile literature.   [1. Earth—Miscellanea.]
I. McLean, Wilson, 1937–   ill.   II. Title.
QB631.4.M55   1998   333.7'2—dc21   98-19053   CIP   AC

•

Sidebars written by Tom Vinciguerra
Book design by Judy Turziano
Photography of original paintings by Bob Hixon
Display typeface, *Blish* by Philip Bouwsma

•

Manufactured in Singapore by CS Graphics
98 99 00   0 9 8 7 6 5 4 3 2 1